How to Dazzle at

Macbeth

Patrick M. Cunningham

 Brilliant Publications

Publisher's information

Published by Brilliant Publications,
1 Church View,
Sparrow Hall Farm,
Edlesborough
Dunstable,
Bedfordshire LU6 2ES.

Tel: 01525 229720
Fax: 01525 229725
Website: www.brilliantpublications.co.uk

Written by Patrick M. Cunningham
Illustrated by Ray and Corrine Burrows
Printed in the UK by Ashford Colour Press Ltd.
© Patrick M. Cunningham
ISBN 1 8976575 93 3
First published 2001
Reprinted 2003
10 9 8 7 6 5 4 3 2

Introduction

The aim of this book is to lead to a deeper understanding of the play through a variety of exercises which will at once stimulate, amuse, and challenge.

There are crosswords, Shakespeare's words, no words (where they are missing with the cloze passages), alternative words and other words to stimulate discussion about the play, either in pairs or larger groups.

The book is intended for teachers of Shakespeare at both KS3 and KS4. There is a range of tasks which crosses the ability range, in particular, the lower ability one. Teachers will find that this book can provide stimulus for assignments.

It is suggested that teachers first go through the play with the 'scene-by-scene' summary and the original text. Then they pick exercises as appropriate for their groups, with possibly the easier, more 'fun' type first, then the more challenging ones as students become more familiar with the play.

Some exercises are ideal as homework tasks. Others are useful for providing stimulus for group work, both oral and written. Answers to some of the sheets are given on page 49.

These work sheets can also be helpful when teaching the drama units of the 'Certificate of Achievement courses in English' for the less able in KS4.

Contents

The somewhat bloody tale of Macbeth

A sentence per scene.

Act 1 Scene 1 To a background of thunder and lightning, three horrible old witches appear on the heath.

Act 1 Scene 2 We hear of the heroic actions of Macbeth and Banquo in battle for King Duncan's forces against the enemy Norwegians.

Act 1 Scene 3 The two heroes meet the witches who flatter Macbeth, saying that one day he will be the king of Scotland.

Act 1 Scene 4 Macbeth hears with some dismay that the king's son will inherit the throne.

Act 1 Scene 5 Lady Macbeth sows seeds in her husband's mind by telling him that he must go for the throne – at any cost.

Act 1 Scene 6 Duncan and his party arrive at the Macbeth castle with little inkling of the treachery about to be unleashed.

Act 1 Scene 7 Lady Macbeth dispels any doubts in her husband's mind – plans for murder are finalized.

Act 2 Scene 1 Macbeth has a vision of a bloody dagger in front of him.

Act 2 Scene 2 Macbeth murders the king while he sleeps.

Act 2 Scene 3 Duncan's body is discovered; Macbeth, supposedly in his fury, kills the 'blood smeared' guards and the king's sons flee the country in fear of their lives.

Act 2 Scene 4 Macduff tells Ross that Scotland has a new king in the shape of Macbeth following Duncan's murder by his grooms.

Act 3 Scene 1 Banquo has suspicions about Macbeth and remembers what the old witches had to say about him being the father of kings.

Act 3 Scene 3 Banquo is killed while his son Fleance escapes with his life.

Act 3 Scene 4 The ghostly form of Banquo appears in Macbeth's place at the banquet – much to the distress of Macbeth.

Act 3 Scene 5   We meet the queen of the witches who prepares for a meeting with Macbeth the following day.

Act 3 Scene 6   Malcolm is in England seeking help to regain the throne.

Act 4 Scene 1   Three apparitions appear to Macbeth with three messages for him: that he need beware of Macduff (Thane of Fife); that no man born of woman will hurt him; and that he will never be defeated until Birnam Wood moves towards Dunsinane.

Act 4 Scene 2   Lady Macduff and her son are brutally murdered.

Act 4 Scene 3   Malcolm and Macduff begin the task of getting a force together to remove the tyrant Macbeth.

Act 5 Scene 1   Lady Macbeth, troubled spiritually, begins to sleepwalk regularly.

Act 5 Scene 2   Forces organized by Scottish noblemen and Malcolm gather in the countryside around Birnam Wood.

Act 5 Scene 3   Macbeth sees his doctor, wishing that the medical man could cure Scotland's disease.

Act 5 Scene 4   Malcolm gets some of his soldiers to cover themselves in branches to fool the enemy about the strength of his numbers.

Act 5 Scene 5   A messenger brings news that Macbeth thought he would never hear – the woods are moving! Malcolm closes in on Macbeth.

Act 5 Scene 6   Malcolm's army prepares to challenge Macbeth at Dunsinane.

Act 5 Scene 7   Young Siward challenges Macbeth and is defeated while Macduff makes his move.

Act 5 Scene 8   Macduff slays Macbeth after telling him that he was born by unnatural means (Caesarean section).

Act 5 Scene 9   Malcolm is hailed king of Scotland as Macbeth's head is carried aloft – the old order has given way to a new, more peaceful order.

Who's who

Draw lines to match the characters with their descriptions.

Malcolm

Egged on by his wife, he murdered the king so that he could take over the throne.

The witches

He was the king of Scotland until he was murdered by dagger.

Macbeth

With Macbeth, he was a leader in Duncan's army. After his death, his ghost came to haunt Macbeth.

Macduff

She was an immoral woman driven by high ambition. She made sure that her husband became king.

Lady Macbeth

He was the eldest son of Duncan. It is the end of the play before he can become the king of Scotland.

Duncan

The killer of Macbeth, he got Malcolm to lead an army against him.

Banquo

These old hags foretold of some events.

Add-on

Practise writing out the names of the people in the play with who they are. Get a friend to test you.

In other words, Macbeth

A translation into modern words.

Part One   Setting the scene

We are taken to a windswept moor. Three evil-looking witches turn up.

First witch   Will we meet again sometime when the weather is pretty 'orrible?

Second witch   It may be when all the fighting has stopped and someone has won and another has lost.

Third witch   That will be before nightfall.

All   Evil may be the winner here! Things which you lot think are good will really be bad. There are going to be one or two nasty things about to 'appen round here. Look out!

The three suddenly disappear in a sound of high-pitched cackles. The mood has been set. We are now taken to a camp near a place called Forres. We meet King Duncan for the first time.

Duncan Tell me the full story, my good sergeant. How did the battle go? I can see you have taken a few blows.

The captain is bleeding a bit.

Captain *(A little breathless and excited.)* Your Highness, I can't praise that man Macbeth enough! He was brilliant in battle and I have rarely seen such bravery on the fields of war. He never thought of his own safety and even though he was outnumbered, he won through. He soon took care of that merciless Macdonwald, I tell you!

The captain is getting more excited by the minute.

He did the decent thing and ripped him apart from head to toe. He claimed his horrible head as a kind of prize. That Macdonwald will certainly never show his face round here again, 'cept on his head impaled on a battlement, that is!

The captain gives a little chuckle as he says these words to the old king.
We have just been given our first indication as to what kind of a man Macbeth is.

Duncan Captain, thank you for that information. I am truly indebted to Macbeth. You too, sir, have done well. Your wounds of battle are indeed honourable. You have fought well and helped to keep the honour of our fair country Scotland. Now, will somebody take this man away to have his wounds treated?

In Scotland there were noblemen who were called thanes. One such thane was a man called Ross. He appears with more news for the king.

Ross I have just come back from Fife. The enemies of our people have hoisted their flag to rub our noses in it. The Norwegians have had the help of a traitor. The thane of Cawdor has helped them in a most shameful fashion. In the end we won through, no thanks to that treacherous Cawdor. I cannot bring myself to mention his name any more!

He gets agitated and spits on the ground.

Duncan Let that noble Macbeth have his title at once! See that the traitor is apprehended and put to death! *He is angry that one of* *his own noblemen should turn traitor.*

We are taken out on the moor again. To the sound of thunder, the three witches appear again. They prattle on about various things, all of which sounds like they are up to no good. To the sound of a drum, Macbeth and his partner-in-arms, a man called Banquo, enter.

Macbeth   I'll tell you something, good friend. This is a foul day indeed!

Banquo   How far is it to Forres? *(He spots the witches.)*
What's this I see? Those three are so wild-looking, it's unbelievable! They look like something from a different planet. Yet here they are on this earth. Look, Macbeth, they have the thin lips of women, yet I'm sure that those are beards they have on their chins! Let's talk to them and see what they are up to.

Macbeth   Speak if you can!

First witch   Hail to you, sir, the thane of Glamis!

Macbeth is indeed the thane of Glamis. It is like being the lord of the manor, as he lives at a place called Glamis Castle.

Second witch   Hail to you sir, thane of Cawdor!

Third witch   All hail Macbeth! You will be king one day!

Banquo   This is something, is it not? You are telling my best friend and fellow fighter that he will have future nobility and a promise of royalty to come? I do not understand all this.

The witches try to depart the scene but Macbeth wants to hear more.

Macbeth   Hey, wait up! What are you on about? I know that I am the thane of Glamis. But how can I be the thane of Cawdor? There is already such a man. He was fighting against our foes, wasn't he Banquo?

Banquo   Did we really see those awful looking figures? Were they in our imagination or what? Maybe, my friend, we have had too much of that drink which makes men mad and see things which are not really there. They told me that my children would be kings! How come? They also told you, my friend Macbeth, that you will be king. Will this really come to pass?

Ross and another thane called Angus arrive to give Macbeth the news that he has indeed got a new title. A constant image throughout the play is that of clothes and their suitability for the wearer. When Macbeth hears of his elevation, he refers to clothes.

Macbeth   Why, Ross, do you call me thane of Cawdor? You are giving me borrowed robes to wear. They are not mine; these robes belong to the real thane of Cawdor.

For possibly the first time in the play, Macbeth lets his thoughts dwell on the prophecies of the old women of the moor. He is conscious of the fact that they had also told Banquo that his children would be kings. Will this cause future problems between them?

Well, maybe I should give this some thought. Is chance going to make me a king? Can I simply become king without any effort on my part?

Banquo   New clothes do not feel comfortable at first. You have to wear them for a while before they become comfortable.

Macbeth   What will be will be! If things are meant to be, then so be it.

Part Two   Growing ambitions

We meet the king's two sons. Some of the words of the king are ironic.

Duncan   How wrong can you be about someone? From the look of him, I would have said that thane of Cawdor was all right. He has let me down badly!

He says this as much in sorrow as in anger.

I put absolute trust in that man, you know.

The question is, will he put the same trust in Macbeth? Macbeth then hears with some dismay that the old king plans to give Malcolm, his eldest son, a title and possibly a royal one at a later date.

Macbeth   How can he make that young upstart the prince of Cumberland? I'll either fail completely or reach the very top! I hope that the stars are not watching! I have these dark and deep desires! Let my eye not see what my hand is planning!

At this point that old saying comes to mind about 'turning a blind eye' to something. At a room in Macbeth's castle, we see Lady Macbeth read a letter from her husband. She is put in the picture and quickly asserts herself so that a plan to kill the old king will soon be hatched.

Lady Macbeth   Come on you spirits! Make sure I have no tender feelings! Make sure that my whole body will be composed of the worst cruelty! Block any passages that lead to remorse! Take away my milk of human kindness!

Macbeth returns, his wife says that Duncan will come to stay with them and she will then put her evil plan into operation. Macbeth is content to follow the plans.

Part Three A bloody deed indeed
The calculating Lady Macbeth orders her husband to act as the perfect host when Duncan and his party arrive as their guests for the big banquet.

Duncan   I must say that this castle is in a nice place. Greetings to you, Lady Macbeth.

Lady Macbeth   Welcome to you, Your Highness. We are at your service and we offer our prayers for your well–being.

Duncan   Where is your husband? He is too fast for us! I think that his goodness and bravery are even better than his speed on a horse! We are, madam, your guests for the night.

Lady Macbeth   We have put our servants at your disposal for the evening.

We move to the feast hall and there are servants carrying lots of food while the guests are entertained with music. It is a jovial atmosphere to which Macbeth contributes a somewhat sombre statement.

Macbeth If we are going to carry out this plan, then it is much better that we do it quickly and get it over with.

We get the impression that his heart is not fully in the plan of murder.

I am his subject and his host tonight. I should be protecting him tonight! Yet am I ambitious enough to want his job? I am like a horse who tries to jump too high and ends up falling on the other side of the fence.

He states his doubts to Lady Macbeth.

Look I do not think that we should go on with this. He has just honoured me with a new title and I know that many people have a good opinion of me.

There is another reference to clothing.

If I carry out this plan, it will be like throwing away new clothes.

Lady Macbeth tears into her husband when he shows signs of wavering. She insults his virility and tells him he is weak. He had uttered the words 'if we should fail' and this was the signal to vent her anger against him. Lady Macbeth does not believe that there is the remotest of chances of failing in the plan.

Lady Macbeth Screw up your courage like the strings of a lute. Its strings are tightened until they are just about to snap. When the king is asleep, I will fill the guards full of wine and give them some merry-making so that their brains will be affected and they will forget their job of looking after the old man. He will be left unguarded and I will see to it that the guards themselves take the blame for his death.

Macbeth remains troubled by the whole business and finds it hard to summon up all his energies for the task.

We are taken to the courtyard of Macbeth's castle. Banquo and his son Fleance are about to retire for the night when they meet Macbeth. Banquo is not that relaxed for someone enjoying the hospitality of a friend. He is still rather troubled by the words of the witches. Macbeth himself is nervous, waiting for the terrible events to unfold. He is having a bit of a private nightmare.

Banquo Ah, Macbeth. Are you still up? Duncan is at rest and very contented it seems. He has given gifts to his hosts and must have really enjoyed his stay with you.

Macbeth bids Banquo goodnight and begins to imagine a few things.

Macbeth Is this a dagger I see in front of me? Is it pointing towards me? *(He's beginning to get agitated.)* Let me hold you! I can see blood as well, dripping from the blade! It was ordered by the gods! Nature itself says that I must do the deed. I will strike like a ghost in the dead of night! My steps will not be heard and no one will know of my whereabouts. When I hear the bell, it will be the signal to send Duncan to either heaven or hell.

Macbeth goes into the sleeping king and the bloody deed is duly done. Macbeth's hands are covered in the king's blood when his wife greets him. She is pleased that he has had the courage to carry through the plan. As far as she is concerned, he has proved his manliness. For Macbeth, there is not quite the same feeling of triumph. He is waking up from a nightmare, but to more troubled thoughts.

Macbeth As I did the stabbing, one of the servants woke up and cried 'murder!' I heard someone say that I wouldn't find it easy to sleep any more. They said that the Thane of Cawdor had murdered sleep as well as the king.

Macbeth is now extremely agitated.

I am afraid to think of what I have just done.

In the meantime, Lady Macbeth is taking charge and is in control of the situation.

Lady Macbeth   I will go and spread the king's blood on to the servants who lie there. Then everyone will think it was them who carried out the murder.

She shows us that she is a scheming kind of person who has seemingly thought of everything to cover her tracks.

Let's go to our chambers. I will wash my hands and that will clear our consciences as well.

Part Four 'We gotta get outa' this place!'

The tension has been high and so there is now a little breather in the action and a little bit of humour from the porter, who cracks a few jokes on the topics of drinking and its effects on various activities. When Macduff asks the porter what three things drink provokes, he replies:

Porter   Sir, it will give you a red nose, it will send you to sleep and it will make you go to the toilet quite a lot.

Will a modern audience recognize all this?

It makes you feel lecherous but reduces the ability to be so. Drink will make men feel virile but they will not be able to do anything about it. It will also make them impotent. To sum up, sir, it is a bit of a liar is drink!

Macduff greets Macbeth and tells him it is time he woke up the king. Lennox refers to the night in terms significant to an Elizabethan audience.

Lennox   It has been a bad night. Chimneys have been blown down and there has been strange-sounding noises in the air. I heard people saying that the earth itself was shaking.

Macbeth   It was indeed a rough night, sure enough.

Lennox   I'm not that old, but I cannot remember a night like this before!

Macduff comes back in, in some state of shock.

Macduff   Horror of horrors! I cannot put words to it! The king has been slain! There has been a most sacrilegious act done here tonight! The one appointed by the Lord has had his life taken away.

There is general chaos all around and Macbeth panics somewhat, adding the king's attendants to his list of victims. He at once arouses Macduff's suspicions. Macbeth tells us that he repents of these sins, yet we do not really believe him. The late king's two sons begin to make their own plans for the immediate future.

Donalbain   *(to his brother)* Let's get away from here before something terrible happens to us as well. We are not quite ready to let our tears flow just yet.

Banquo   We must look into this terrible act further. We should not be afraid, for God will help us find the truth. It has been a most treacherous act.

Malcolm   *(to his brother)* Let us not hang around here and mix with this company. False men pretend that they are sorrowful. I'll go to England at once!

Donalbain   I'll go to Ireland. It is better we keep apart. When some men smile at you, you can almost see the dagger behind it!

The two then depart. They know that things are not so good and they do not really trust anyone around here at the moment.

Ross and an old man discuss the recent events and this adds to the whole feeling that something terrible is happening. It may even be something unnatural. Throughout this play, there is a feeling of the unnatural and the fact that the world is rather upside down. Remember the earlier words 'fair is foul and foul is fair'. Even the late king's horses must have suspected something was not right. Ross tells us that they broke out of their stalls. Macduff tells us of the actions of the late king's sons.

Macduff   The king's sons have fled this place. Maybe they are involved in the killing.

Ross   Will Macbeth now become King of Scotland?

Part Five   Who invited the ghost?

There is a celebration banquet at Forres with Macbeth as the new king saying to his wife that Banquo is the chief guest. Banquo is not very happy; he suspects Macbeth very strongly of having become king by evil skulduggery. He also still harbours ambitions for himself, remembering the witches' prophecies.

Banquo   *(upon entering a room in the palace)* You *(meaning Macbeth)* have it all now. You are Cawdor, Glamis, all, like those strange women foretold. I fear that you did not receive these titles by good means! Your sons should not inherit your crown. The witches also told me that my sons would be kings.

There's a procession as Macbeth and his entourage enter. Banquo pledges loyalty to the king. He makes plans to leave but says he will return for the feast.

Macbeth   I hear that Duncan's two sons are out of Scotland, fled to Ireland and England. Perhaps they had something to do with the murder. Banquo, when you come back, we have important business to discuss. Is Fleance *(Banquo's son)* going with you?

Soon Macbeth is alone and he reveals a few of his thoughts to us.

Macbeth Banquo is a person of a very noble quality. He is also clever and this could be a danger to my position. I remember how he reacted when the old women called me king. Then, didn't they tell him that he would be the father of kings? My crown is a little useless without children! I have gone to the bother of getting rid of Duncan only for this man to take over!

Are we seeing the real Macbeth here? Is this the noble man of the opening action?

Banquo will have to be eliminated! And that son of his! His inheritors must also perish.

Macbeth talks to his hired assassins who are to carry out his plan to be rid of Banquo. The deed (yet another bloody one) will be done before night fall.
In another room Macbeth talks to his wife, not revealing everything about his plans.

Macbeth We have injured goodness, not killed it off completely. If it was a snake, she would be injured, not dead and ready to heal.

This seems to confirm for us the kind of person Macbeth really is. He has made himself a kind of champion for the forces of evil.

On a road leading to the palace, Banquo is attacked and killed. His son Fleance manages to escape. Banquo recognises the peril and it is the final awful confirmation of what he suspected.

Banquo Oh, the treachery of this! Get you gone, Fleance! I want you to get revenge for all this!

It is the last time we see Banquo alive. However, we are not completely finished with him just yet. The state banquet begins and there is an extra guest. Only Macbeth can see him. The uninvited guest is the ghost of Banquo. Is he there to prod the conscience of the man who arranged for him to be killed? Lady Macbeth notices her husband's strange behaviour and his mood is not helped by being told that Fleance has escaped.

Macbeth   *(to the ghost)* What is this? You are hardly human form! You have no marrow in your bones. Your blood is cold. Just who are you?

Soon afterwards, Lady Macbeth sends all the guests away and the party is finished abruptly. A little while after, Macbeth confesses that he is slightly troubled by all the recent events.

Macbeth   I am steeped in blood. I have such strange things in my head just now. I cannot sleep very easily.

Part Six   The untouchable?

In another room in the palace, a couple of lords are talking about things as they are now. They tell us that Macduff has gone to England to join Malcolm in getting together with the 'pious' King Edward to bring some kind of order back to Scotland. The English king seems to be the complete opposite of Macbeth. One of the lords remarks that he wouldn't mind some meat on the tables, banquets free from knives, and honours given out on merit alone. He is summing up for us what the country appears to be like under Macbeth.

Meanwhile Macbeth has another date with the witches on the moor.

All the witches together

        Double, double toil and trouble: fire burn and cauldron bubble.

Another set of superstitions is about to be laid before us. They are literally throwing everything into the pot (cauldron) and making some kind of an evil spell. They conjure up some apparitions to deliver another message to Macbeth. The first of the apparitions appears with an armed head.

1st apparition   Macbeth, you will have to be very wary of the thane of Fife!

The audience knows that the thane of Fife is none other than Macduff. So does Macbeth.

Macbeth   Thanks for warning me. I knew that man would be up to no good against me!

2nd apparition   Macbeth, be bold and strong. You can laugh at mere mortals of men because no one who has been born of woman can harm you.

Macbeth   Well that's all right then! Macduff, you were born of a woman, so you cannot touch me, can you? I can let you live then. I am untouchable!

We are not quite finished with predictions just yet. To the sound of thunder, a third apparition makes an appearance. It too will have something to say to Macbeth.

3rd apparition   Macbeth, be lion-hearted. Don't worry about conspirators. You will never be defeated until the wood which lies about a dozen miles from here moves towards Dunsinane Hill.

Macbeth   That's all right then. This can never happen! I am safe. No one can harm me now!

The witches have one more image for Macbeth. They conjure up an image of Banquo smiling in a knowing way at him.

Macbeth   *(thinking out loud for us)* I will act quickly! You are lost if you delay in plans. I will go to the castle of Macduff to surprise them there! Macduff's wife and babes must die by sword!

It is now clear to the audience what kind of man Macbeth really is. Is it necessary for the family of Macduff to be killed? After all, those apparitions told him he had nothing to worry about! Surely he is now an untouchable person in no danger? Can this be the same 'brave Macbeth' seen in the opening scenes?

Macduff   *(is he describing the same person?)* There was never a more evil devil than Macbeth. You could scour hell and not find anything more evil.

Unlike the earlier murders, these are shocking because they are without motive. Macduff is ready to rise to the occasion and, with some help, save his country which has become like a sick patient (about to die?).

Part Seven   Take a bough, Your Royal Highness
The final showdown

We will soon be bidding farewell to Lady Macbeth. She will not be around to witness the climax to the action of this bloody play. We see a woman unlike the one from the early part of the action.

Lady Macbeth   My hands will never be clean! All the perfumes of the East will never purify my hand.

This, we need to remind ourselves, is the same lady who earlier had said that she and her husband could wipe away the guilt of murder by simply washing their hands.

> Banquo's dead and gone. He cannot come out of his grave!

She has taken to sleepwalking and is probably seeing things. Maybe she could blame her husband for lack of sleep! Didn't he, earlier, 'murder sleep'? Along with a lot of people as well!

The action now moves to the final confrontation. The army to take on Macbeth is approaching. At Dunsinane there is a discussion of the strength of the two sides.

Angus   *(another of the many thanes now lined up against Macbeth)* Macbeth's had it, you know! *(to another thane called Caithness)* His army people only listen to him because he is their commander, not from devotion to him. He wears clothes that are too big for him! He has the robe of a giant, yet he is a mere dwarf.

The image of clothing was mentioned before. Angus thinks that Macbeth is not fit to wear the clothes of the office of king of Scotland.

Caithness   We will obey the true leader, who is Malcolm. We will give our last drop of blood to save this land from the tyranny it has suffered.

Lennox   *(a third thane present here)* We will drown the weeds and give room for the flowers to grow.

We see Macbeth in a room in his castle.

Macbeth   I know that there are people out to get me. *(defiantly)* I will be all right! They told me that I could not be beaten! The wood will never move and Malcolm was born of a woman! I will not go rotten with fear. Now, tell me, doctor, how is my good wife?

Doctor   Alas, like the country. Not in good shape at all. There would be no profit for me in this patient.

The action moves to Birnam Wood where Malcolm and his army are drawing ever closer to Macbeth. Malcolm has a way of making trees take legs and walk!

Malcolm   Let every one of my men take a bough and cover himself with it. Move with the branches in front of you and it will appear as if the whole wood is moving.

The battle is at its height and Macbeth receives news of his wife's death. He also hears the rather disturbing news that a wood is on its way.

Macbeth   Our castle is strong enough to survive a siege. We will hold up and the attackers will die of famine before we give up.

A messenger arrives.

Macbeth   What have you come to tell me? Get it out quickly!

Messenger   I don't quite know how to tell you this. I do not know how it is so, but as I stood on the hill and looked towards Birnam, I could swear that I saw the wood move.

Macbeth rants at him calling him a liar and a slave.

We are now in full battle. Malcolm has Macduff and old Siward with him.

Malcolm   Now that you are near Macbeth's castle, throw down your boughs and show yourselves as soldiers. You are a worthy man, Macduff. Go for it! We shall do what we have to do, according to our plan of operation.

The battle continues on the plain near the castle and Macbeth manages to kill Siward's son. Macbeth makes reference to one of the predictions.

Macbeth   I'll fight like a bear under threat! Where is the man who was not born of a woman?

Macduff seeks out Macbeth.

Macduff   Show your face, tyrant! I will get revenge for my wife and children!

Siward leads him to the castle telling him that it has surrendered peaceably.

Macbeth   I am not going to be like the Roman fool who gives up when he is captured. *(He is in defiant mood)* I won't fall on my own sword!

Macduff   Turn, hell hound, turn!

Macbeth   I have taken enough of your blood already.

Macduff   I have no words for you. My sword will do the talking for me.

They fight. Macbeth is killed and Macduff claims his prize, the head of his enemy. Macduff salutes Malcolm as king. The new king gives a speech about how the country has been saved and how harmony will replace tyranny. He leaves for a coronation ceremony at Scone.

Visit the brain gym

Complete the word grid below. All the clues contain anagrams of the answers. The anagrams are set in bold.

Across

1. **E CHEAT** for the witches' leader.

2. **SET FOR** a place like Birnam – not moving!

5. **RUN LOAD C** for a pot for the witches to brew up some trouble.

7. **HEAT N** the title for a Scottish nobleman.

9. **O MC MALL** for the son of a king.

Down

1. **THE HA** is a place where the witches met.

3. **MOST R** was brewing with thunder and lightning as the witches met.

4. **NO QUAB** for a ghostly person.

6. **ADD E** for the condition of a king.

8. **LIVE** for being wicked like Macbeth.

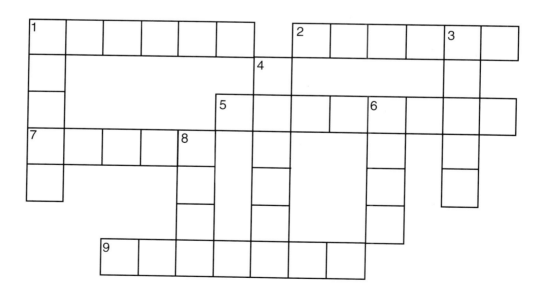

Add-on

Try these anagrams too:

dremur, raCdow, enisDuann, caLM thebday.

Who are these Scottish people then?

From the clues, find them on the grid.

D	O	N	A	L	B	A	I	N	N
H	T	E	B	C	A	M	G	O	G
G	C	D	N	M	A	L	R	L	Y
Y	H	O	R	C	U	O	J	G	Z
N	E	H	D	I	S	C	B	G	I
O	S	U	L	S	Q	L	A	S	U
Y	F	V	F	L	E	A	N	C	E
F	Q	I	B	O	J	M	Q	C	V
N	I	R	N	A	C	N	U	D	D
F	S	J	I	Y	K	F	O	C	W

- ◆   Son of a king – he fled to Ireland
- ◆   Son of Banquo – he escaped death
- ◆   He was murdered while he slept
- ◆   This man finally killed Macbeth
- ◆   Son of a king – later became one
- ◆   His ghost turned up at a banquet
- ◆   One of the Scottish noblemen
- ◆   This man had 'vaulting ambition'

Add-on

What animal is Shakespeare thinking of when he writes 'I have no spur
To prick the sides of my intent, but only Vaulting Ambition'? (Act 1 Scene 7)

A word (or eight!) about Macbeth

All eight missing words are found on the grid.

A	M	B	I	T	I	O	N	Z	Z
Y	Y	G	X	R	W	A	T	D	Y
D	E	J	T	O	K	S	X	F	C
S	L	F	M	U	L	P	A	M	B
L	D	A	D	B	E	T	E	B	S
O	N	G	P	L	H	E	M	S	Y
D	A	G	G	E	R	E	T	A	W
T	Q	W	R	H	E	A	G	W	M
K	Z	U	T	M	W	L	P	T	J
Z	S	F	Z	R	L	X	S	U	D

It's a tale of 'vaulting _____' when _____ witches helped to sow the seeds for this with their predictions to Macbeth on the moor as he returns from battle, covered in glory. The 'old hags' speak almost in riddles. They help to spread a feeling of evil with lines such as:

Double, double, toil and _____ .

One of the main players in the action is a _____ called Lady Macbeth. She has a large part to play in the murder of a king with a _____ while he slept in her home.

This same lady later tries to wash away her guilt with _____ and her _____ pattern is also disturbed. She takes to walking around instead of sleeping!

She appears to be very evil. However, she did say that the old king reminded her of her _____ . This is a brief moment of tenderness in this tale of treachery and betrayal.

Who am I?

Work out the answers going across and my identity will be revealed.

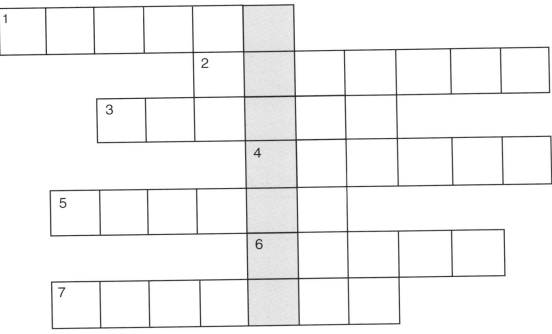

1. Could it be that the trees in this wood really did move? (6)

2. He was the son of a murdered king (7)

3. This old king fell victim to evil treachery (6)

4. His ghost certainly spoiled someone's meal (6)

5. A murder weapon (6)

6. A noble title in Scotland (5)

7. Did this threesome brew up some evil on the heath? (7)

Add-on

The hidden person has several titles in the play. Can you list them?

Good news week?

Fill in the answers on the grid and you will reveal a message in the shaded area – good news by the end of the play?

1. By the end of the play, who was the king? (7)

2. At the beginning of the play, who was the king? (6)

3. What country were they king of? (8)

4. Who fought bravely in battle with Macbeth? (6)

5. What did Lady Macbeth want, to help 'clear us of this deed'? (5)

6. What threesome did Macbeth meet on the moor?

7. Where did Macbeth meet them? (5)

8. What was 'vaulting' for Macbeth? (8)

9. What appeared to move? (6)

10. Whose wife and son were killed? (Macbeth to blame?) (7)

11. Which son of Banquo escaped death just in time? (7)

12. What 'thane of' did Macbeth become early on in the play? (6)

13. What instrument was used to kill the old king? (6)

What's it all about?

Work out each answer, fill in the grid and read what you see on the left.

1. Unlawful killing – this certainly happened in the play. (6)

2. Losing your temper? There is a lot of this in the play. (5)

3. It means having bottle – shown in some battles? (7)

4. Many of these in the play – in one, Macbeth showed himself to be brave. (7)

5. Lady Macbeth was this – it's wicked! (4)

6. It goes with lightning and could be heard as the witches were on the heath. (7)

7. The opposite of love – did some people have this feeling for Lady Macbeth? (6)

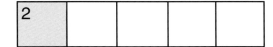

Macbeth

Fill in the 10 answers to the following.

1. The Thane of _____ , turned traitor against the king in battles with invading enemies at the beginning of the play? (6) _____

2. He was a friend and fellow member of the king's army with Macbeth, but was later murdered, his ghost coming back to do some haunting! (6)

    _____

3. His brother was called Malcolm. His father was king, for some time at least. (9)

    _____

4. The place where the witches met. (4) _____

5. The king of Scotland murdered by Macbeth. He was true and generous. (6)

    _____

6. It was the murder weapon. (6) _____

7. The name of the castle where Macbeth and his scheming wife lived. (6)

    _____

8. This 'character' in the play is a kind of messenger and commentator on events. (4) _____

9. This word was used to describe Macbeth and his friend after the enemy's defeat at the beginning of the play. (5) _____

10. The three of them told Macbeth that one day he would be king. (7)

    _____

Add-on

How many witches? How many apparitions? How many murderers?

When shall we three meet again?

Find the 15 Shakespeare words found in the play that are represented by the more modern word (or words) below.

Down

1. Confusion (5,5 with a hyphen in the play)
2. Murder (5)
3. A sort of cat (10)
4. Handle (7)
6. Skin (4)
10. Entranced (4)
13. 'I am coming'(4)

Across

3. Stomach (4)
5. Before (3)
7. Bitterness (4)
8. More (3)
9. Cowardly (4,6 hyphen and apostrophe in the play)
11. Clothes (6)
12. Yes (3)
14. Darling (6)

Solve it!

Fill in the answers on the next page and reveal a description of the play.

1. They told Macbeth he would be safe as long as the trees didn't move – but beware Macduff! (11)
2. Plenty of this red stuff was spilled (5)
3. She helped convince her husband that he should be the king of Scotland. (4,7)
4. A description of Duncan, perhaps? (3,4)
5. A description of Birnam Wood by the final act of the play, perhaps? Maybe it's just in the imagination! (2,3,4)
6. Where did the trees move towards? (9)
7. Complete this quote directed at Macbeth – an indication of what's to come? '_____ shall be king' (3)
8, 9 and 10. The natural happenings while the three witches come on the stage at first. (7,3,9)
11. Which country did Malcolm flee to? (7)
12. Complete the quote: 'None _____ born shall harm Macbeth' (2,5)
13. What was Banquo's son called? (6)
14. He turned traitor early on in the action. (5,2,6)
15. He was a Scottish nobleman. (4)
16. The word used by Shakespeare meaning 'before' as in '___ the set of sun' (3)
17. An accurate description of Macbeth? (1,6)
18. Pot into which the witches threw many things for a heady brew of ambition and disloyalty. (8)
19. She was the old hags' leader. (6)
20. Could this describe Macbeth's actions? (4,3,6)
21. What kind of fool wouldn't Macbeth play? (5)
22. He was eventually to take the crown. (5,7)

Add-on

Imagine that Macbeth was keeping a diary. Write down his entry for the day he returned from battle with the Norwegians.

13 steps to finish Macbeth

Answer all 14 questions, starting at the bottom and finishing at the top.
The final word means just that!

1. Did this 'character' have a body? He turned up at a feast! (5,2,6)
2. Description of Macbeth, by Malcolm at the end. (4,7)
3. Who scornfully says 'we fail?' in Act 1? (4,7)
4. Banquo's description of the witches at the opening of Act 3. (5,5)
5. Shakespeare's words for 'confusion' in the opening act (5,5)
6. The name of one of King Duncan's two sons (9)
7. Two opposite sounding words spoken by the witches. (4,4)
8. What people such as Macduff, Ross and Lennox are. (8)
9. Who kills Macbeth in the end? (7)
10. A word which could describe Macbeth's rise to the throne. (7)
11. What crime did King Duncan suffer from?(6)
12. Complete the missing word: ___ of Cawdor (5)
13. This person sits on a throne: Duncan? Macbeth? Malcolm? (4)
14. Conclusion: Malcolm on the throne after death of Macbeth.(3)

Add-on

Write a few sentences describing the character of Macbeth.

Happy families?

Find the 20 missing words. Take them from the word bank below.

It is Scotland. A man called Duncan is the _____ of Scotland. Two of his

generals have fought _____ in battle for him. Their names are

_____ and _____ . The _____ of Cawdor has become a

traitor, so Macbeth is to be given his title. However, he has set his sights on a far

more important title and by the end of the action he will have taken the _____

by force. By then, he will have a lot of _____ on his hands. King Duncan

intends for his son _____ to inherit the throne, but this does not happen.

When King Duncan is murdered with a _____ , his sons Malcolm and

_____ flee the country in fear of their lives. His murder is a terrible act

of _____ , presumed to have been committed by his erstwhile loyal

soldier. However, the hand that sank the weapon into Duncan was guided by a

certain woman, known as _____ Macbeth.

During the action, we see a lot of the three old _____ who constantly

harp on about the future and victory for the forces of _____ . They have met on

a desolate _____ where they make certain _____ about what

will happen.

Duncan is killed after a banquet. Banquo is also murdered. His _____ later

'appears' to stir someone's conscience. By the end, Duncan's son and younger

brother will have victory. Before that happens, a whole _____ appears to

move. In the end, the country is restored to some _____ after a rather bad

time. It seems that the forces for _____ have finally triumphed, despite all.

Word bank					
Macbeth	**bravely**	**Donalbain**	**moor**	**Malcolm**	**good**
Banquo	**ghost**	**treachery**	**Lady**	**forest**	**evil**
dagger	**thane**	**peace**	**witches**	**throne**	**king**
predictions	**blood**				

Tell us the story of Macbeth

Read the following sentences about the play. Then write them out in the correct order of the story.

- Macbeth meets some spirits who tell him a few things which make him think himself invincible.

- The dastardly deed is done whilst the old king is a guest of the Macbeths.

- We meet the three weird witches for the first time on a desolate Scottish moor.

- In the meantime, Lady Macduff and her son are the latest victims of the blood-letting.

- A wood appears to be moving towards Macbeth. His enemies close in for the kill.

- Meanwhile, two generals in Duncan's army have just helped see off the enemy forces to earn praise from the grateful king.

- Banquo is the next to die as the country goes into a bad state under Macbeth.

- Macbeth is slain and Malcolm assumes power to the great joy of the country.

- One of these generals has an ambition leading him to plot with his wife to murder Duncan and take the throne as king of Scotland.

- Malcolm and Donalbain flee the country in the aftermath of the murder of their father.

An A to Z of Shakespeare's Macbeth

Give answers to the following.

A	means 'I am coming'.	_____
B	a nobleman who fought with Macbeth?	_____
C	was a boiling one at the start of Act 4.	_____
D	brutally murdered by a dagger?	_____
E	Shakespeare uses for 'haste'?	_____
F	escaped as his dad was murdered?	_____
G	a cat mentioned by a witch early on?	_____
H	is the only witch to be named.	_____
I	place where one of Duncan's sons fled?	_____
J	means 'risk'.	_____
K	Duncan's title before he was murdered?	_____
L	pushes her husband to seek the throne?	_____
M	loses his family to the evils of Macbeth?	_____
N	defeated in battle at the beginning?	_____
O	was an owl.	_____
P	told funny tales of what drink can do to you?	_____
Q	is Shakespeare's word for murder.	_____
R	brings messages and describes events of the play?	_____
S	did Macbeth find hard to get after a murder?	_____
T	the title for a Scottish nobleman?	_____
U	describes the chin of someone not bearded.	_____
V	another name for courage shown in battle?	_____
W	on the heath to tell Macbeth his future?	_____
X	probably not played at the fateful banquet?	_____
Y	the son of the earl of Northumberland?	_____
Z	may well describe the amount of joy in the country under Macbeth's rule.	_____

All change for Macbeth

Copy out the passages replacing the word (or words) in bold with a word (or words) from the word bank at the end. The final story will have the same meaning.

Part one

We have indeed a **tale** of treachery, personal ambition and lust for power. The hero of war who returned from foreign lands will have changed before the end of the action into an evil, sadistic **butcher**. Macbeth has earned praise from **his king**, only to turn against him before long.

We open with Macbeth and **his fellow soldier** meeting three **old hags** on a desolate moor. If the conqueror of the Norwegians had not met these brewers of evil, would the outcome of the story have been the same?

They **told** him that he would be king of **his country** as well as thane of Cawdor. All the time, fuelling his ambition was **his wife.** She urged him to go for it. She didn't have any **qualms** about killing to achieve their aims and goaded her husband about his manhood when he harboured doubts about the whole idea. Blocking the way is King Duncan. The old man is duly invited to **the Macbeths' home** and suffers the ultimate in back-stabbing when he is murdered with a most deadly dagger – would that have been the same one Macbeth thought he had seen in his dreams some time before?

Word bank

Glamis Castle	doubts	story	killer	Scotland
Lady Macbeth	informed	Banquo	witches	Duncan

Part two

Soon after the **dastardly** deed is done, **Duncan's two sons** flee the country in fear of their own lives. Scotland has a new king; this does not **spell** good times. Banquo recalls the words of the old women on the moor (the same old women he thought looked more like men with their beards) when they told him that his sons would be kings. Does this make him a rival to **his one-time brother in arms**? Suspicions are proved true and he too dies soon afterwards, also callously murdered.

Revenge **quickly** occurs when the ghostly shape of Banquo appears at a banquet to **torment** Macbeth, who by now has quite a bit of blood on his hands. Is he seeing things? Whatever the facts, the banquet is quickly abandoned. However, we have not seen the last of **ghostly things**. Another meeting on the moor and Macbeth is told three things, two of which will make him rest more easy. He is told that no woman born of man will ever **defeat** him and that he will never be beaten until **a certain forest** starts moving. He is also told to beware of a certain person, **the thane of Fife**. This is good advice…

Word bank					
Macduff	spirits	Macbeth	horrify	evil	soon
mean	Birnam Wood		overthrow	Malcolm and Donalbain	

Part three

The body count rises **again** as Macduff's wife and son are **brutally** murdered. Again, a certain man who has, by now, become something of a tyrant is involved even if it's not his own hand that has carried out the **deed**. Scotland is in a bad way and something has to be done to sort it out. Malcolm and Macduff are busy getting a force together to speed up this process. The former has sought help from the **king of England**. Meanwhile, Lady Macbeth has started to sleepwalk, weighed down heavily by her conscience. The earlier prediction by her husband that they would sleep no more is proving to be quite accurate. At the same time, Macbeth wishes that his **medical man** could cure his country's disease. Before long it is all over for **our one-time hero**. Malcolm makes his forces appear larger in number as they hide behind branches and storm towards **Macbeth's castle**. Macduff (born after a Caesarean operation) **slays** his former friend and, to the general relief of Scotland, Malcolm becomes **king** – a **triumph** for good over evil.

Word bank				
victory	Macbeth	cruelly	monarch	Edward
once more	Dunsinane	doctor	kills	act

He's lost his head

Can you put these four events into the correct order in which they happened during the play?

- There is much joy in Scotland as Malcolm becomes king following Macbeth's death.

- With his wife urging him on, Macbeth decides that Duncan should be killed.

- Macbeth proves to be a brave fighter as he helps defeat the enemy forces.

- With Duncan out of the way, Macbeth leads Scotland into misery and chaos.

Step one
_____

_____
Step two
_____

_____
Step three
_____

_____
Step four
_____

_____

Draw a scene from the play.

Silent in Glamis Castle

Fill in the missing words. Each one contains a silent letter.

The play opens on a heath with three _____ mumbling strange words

about 'bubble' and 'trouble'. At first Macbeth is like the proverbial _____

in shining armour when he and Banquo helped see off the enemy forces. Then he

starts to _____ to others too much. First he hears the old hags tell him he

will be king one day. Then he hears his wife egging him on with a _____ to

kill King Duncan and seize the throne. It is a little like _____ to the slaughter

when Duncan is stabbed to death as he sleeps in Macbeth's _____. Any

hopes that Scotland will be a peaceful place are soon _____. Macbeth

proves to be a tyrant and an old pal returns in the shape of a _____ to give

him no _____ of comfort. Soon Macbeth is under pressure and before

the end of the play the forces of Macduff and _____ make sure that he

is defeated. His head is paraded around as a kind of symbol of the end of tyranny.

Shakespeare's words

Give another word with the same meaning.

spongy _____

dunnes _____

hargbinger _____

ere _____

trifles _____

broil _____

dudgeon _____

Greymalkin _____

valour's minion _____

hurly-burly _____

quell _____

gouts _____

rapt withal _____

attire _____

chamberlains _____

Paddock _____

suborn'd _____

Scale of dragon, tooth of wolf

Double, double, toil and trouble

Fire burn and cauldron bubble

The voice of Scotland

Use the newspaper–style headlines below and write your own report to feature on the front page of a different daily.

Scottish Daily Gazette
LATE EDITION

THE TRIAL OF THE CENTURY
Lady Macbeth breaks down as she tells of 'sleepless nights'

Scottish Daily News

King Duncan Assassinated

Scotland was thrown into chaos and disarray last night after her elderly King Duncan was brutally murdered. The assassins reputedly knifed the king to death while he was asleep in Glamis Castle, the home of the Macbeths.

THE SCOTTISH HIGHLANDER

The agony then the ecstasy

The country was finally celebrating last night after a bloody battle inside Dunsinane Castle where the much disliked dictatator Macbeth was defeated. Bonfires were being lit and people were taking to the streets in droves for impromptu parties to celebrate the end of this gloomy period.

The things they said

Find out who spoke these lines and the meaning of the words spoken. The lines are in the correct order of being spoken in the play.

Act One

When the hurly-burly's done,
When the battle's lost and won.

_____
_____
_____

So foul and fair a day I have not seen.

_____
_____
_____

All hail Macbeth! that shalt be king
hereafter.

_____
_____
_____

You shall be king.

_____
_____
_____

The Thane of Cawdor lives: why do you
dress me
In borrowed robes?

_____
_____
_____
_____

Like our strange garments, cleave not to their mould _____
But with the aid of use.

_____
_____

He was a gentleman on whom I built
An absolute trust.

_____
_____
_____
_____

Come, you spirits
That tend on mortal thoughts, unsex me here,
And fill me, from the crown to the toe, top-full
Of direst cruelty! make thick my blood,
Stop up th'access and passage to remorse,

_____
_____
_____
_____
_____

Yet do I fear thy nature;   _____

It is too full o' the milk of human kindness   _____

To catch the nearest way.   _____

    _____

If it were done, when 'tis done, then 'twere   _____

    well

It were done quickly: ...   _____

... I have no spur   _____

To prick the sides of my intent, but only   _____

Vaulting ambition, which o'erleaps itself,   _____

And fall on th'other.   _____

We fail?   _____

    _____

Away, and mock the time with fairest show: _____

False face must hide what the false heart   _____

doth know.   _____

Act Two

Is this a dagger which I see before me,   _____

The handle toward my hand?   _____

Come let me clutch thee.   _____

    _____

He could not miss 'em. Had he not resembled   _____

My father as he slept, I had done't.   _____

    _____

Glamis hath murdered sleep, and therefore Cawdor   _____

Shall sleep no more: Macbeth shall sleep no more!   _____

    _____

I am afraid to think what I have done.   _____

I'll gild the faces of the grooms withal;
For it must seem their guilt.

_____
_____
_____

A little water clears us of this deed.

_____

Act Three

Thou has it now: King, Cawdor, Glamis, all
As the weird women promis'd; and I fear,
Thou play'dst most foully for't.

_____
_____
_____

There is none but he
Whose being I do fear; and under him
My genius is rebuk'd, as it is said,
Mark Antony's was by Caesar.

_____
_____
_____
_____

We have scorch'd the snake, not kill'd it:
She'll close and be herself, whilst our poor malice
Remains in danger of her former tooth.

_____
_____

O, treachery! Fly, good Fleance, fly, fly, fly!
Thou mayst revenge. O slave!

_____
_____

You lack the season of all natures, sleep.

_____
_____

Look on't again I dare not.

_____
_____

Act Four

Double, double, toil and trouble;
Fire burn and cauldron bubble.

_____
_____
_____
_____

Be bloody, bold, and resolute; laugh to scorn _____

The power of man, for none of woman born _____

Shall harm Macbeth.   _____

                                           _____

Macbeth shall never vanquish'd be until   _____

Great Birnam Wood to high Dunsinane Hill   _____

Shall come against him.   _____

                                           _____

The very firstlings of my heart shall be   _____

The firstlings of my hand.   _____

                                           _____

I would not be the villain that thou think'st. _____

                                           _____

Macbeth   _____

is ripe for shaking, and the powers above _____

Put on their instruments.   _____

                                           _____

Act Five

It is an accustomed action with her, to seem _____

thus washing her hands.   _____

                                           _____

What need we fear who knows it, when   _____

none can call our power to account?   _____

Yet who would have thought the old man   _____

to have had so much blood in him?   _____

                                           _____

What, will these hands ne'er be clean?   _____

                                           _____

Those he commands move only in command, _____

Nothing in love; now does he feel his title _____

Hang loose about him, like a giant's robe _____

Upon a dwarfish thief. _____

_____

Why should I play the Roman fool, and die _____

On mine own sword? whiles I see lives, _____

the gashes _____

Do better upon them. _____

_____

Hail, king! for so thou art. _____

_____

Act one   **Act two**

Act four   **Act five**

Add-on

Can you remember one of the witches' potions?